Stephen By Andrew

A Second Look at the Gospel

Proclaimed By Dr. Stephen Cook
at Second Baptist Church, Memphis,
2010 to 2015

ANDREW SMITH

© 2016
Published in the United States by Nurturing Faith, Inc., Macon, GA,
www.nurturingfaith.net.

Library of Congress Cataloging-in-Publication Data is available.

ISBN 978-1-938514-98-2

All rights reserved. Printed in the United States of America.

*Unless otherwise indicated, scripture quotations are taken
from the New Revised Version of the Bible.*

Interior and cover design by Amy C. Cook
Cover photo as well as "Challenge" photo courtesy of Carol P. Mathis

Contents

Foreword xi

Preface xv

Assurance

1. The Pause Button 4
   (Matthew 17:4)

2. Nowhere 6
   (Exodus 17:3)

3. Goodness and Mercy 8
   (Psalm 23:6)

4. Green Pastures 10
   (Psalm 23:2)

5. Difficulties 12
   (Revelation 21:3-4)

6. Transformed 16
   (Romans 12:2)

7. Even at the Grave 18
   (Psalm 22:23-24)

8. Remember 20
   (1 John 5:2)

9. Understanding 22
   (Psalm 8:3)

10. To Strive..24
    (Philippians 3:14)

11. Thanksgiving..26
    (Matthew 6:33)

12. The Same Mind...28
    (Philippians 2:5)

13. In All Things...30
    (1 Thessalonians 5:18)

14. Courage..32
    (Acts 3:1-4)

15. Circumstances..34
    (Genesis 39:12)

16. The Devil and the Deep Red Sea..............36
    (Exodus 13:21; 14:9, 13)

17. Face to Face..38
    (1 John 3:2)

18. Reality..40
    (Mark 1:17)

LOVE ... HOPE ... JOY

19. Joseph and God..44
    (Matthew 1:19-20, 24-25)

20. Blessed...46
    (Matthew 4:25-5:2)

21. Salt...48
    (Matthew 5:13)

22. The Fight..50
    (Matthew 5:22)

23. Choose..52
    (Genesis 2:15; 3:6, 23)

24. A Living Hope..54
    (1 Peter 1:3)

25. Leave!..56
    (John 14:2)

26. Weeds...58
    (Matthew 13:24-25)

27. Fair...60
    (Matthew 20:16)

28. The Table..62
    (Ephesians 4:4-6)

29. Where Is Joy?..64
    (Mark 9:2, 5)

30. Wonder...66
    (Psalm 19:1)

31. Declare the Word..68
    (Psalm 119:11-13)

32. Hosanna!...70
    (Mark 11:9)

33. Gifts..72
    (1 Corinthians 12:4)

34. That Woman..74
    (John 4:7)

35. Limits..76
    (John 6:42)

36. Mindset...78
    (Romans 8:6)

37. The Made-up Mind..80
    (John 7:41, 52)

38. Hope and Suffering...82
    (Romans 5:2)

39. The Choice...84
    (Joshua 24:15)

40. The Light..86
    (John 12:23)

41. Because..88
    (Mark 16:8)

Challenge

42. Get Ready..92
    (Matthew 3:1-2)

43. Darkness and Light..94
    (Isaiah 60:1)

44. Worry...96
    (Matthew 6:34)

45. Bones...98
    (Ezekiel 36:4)

46. Who Is Not My Neighbor?..100
    (Luke 10:29)

47. Touched..102
    (Mark 1:40-41)

48. Wilderness Time 104
    (Mark 1:12)

49. The Lame Man..106
    (Acts 4:13)

50. Horror of Horrors...108
    (Acts 8:12)

51. Success..110
    (Mark 10:37)

52. Using Sight..112
    (Mark 10:46-49, 51-52)

53. Gathered..114
    (Isaiah 43:9)

54. Yes, But..116
    (Jeremiah 1:6-7, 8)

55. Mary's Perfume...118
    (John 12:3)

56. Tags..120
    (John 9:8)

57. Imitators..122
    (Ephesians 1-2)

58. Unique...124
    (1 Samuel 17:39)

59. Called..126
   (Genesis 12:8)

60. Afraid...128
   (Luke 1:30)

61. New Truth..130
   (Acts 19:3)

SERVICE

62. Jesus and the Good Old Boys..........................134
   (Matthew 4:19)

63. Watch Out...136
   (Acts 1:5)

64. Washed Feet..138
   (John 13:5)

65. Grace..142
   (2 Corinthians 9:7-8)

66. Doing...144
   (1 Corinthians 13:1-2)

67. Who Is Calling? 146
   (1 Samuel 3:10)

68. Unity..148
   (Acts 4:32)

69. The Gift...150
   (Acts 3:6)

70. Be Careful..152
   (Deuteronomy 8:11)

71. Stones of Remembrance................................154
   (Joshua 1:9; 4:2-3)

72. Change..156
   (Matthew 2:1-3)

73. Easter People...158
   (Luke 24:52)

74. The Cross..160
   (John 19:25)

75. Take Off Your Shoes....................................162
   (Exodus 3:3)

76. Carefully...164
   (Mark 1:30-31)

77. Waiting...166
   (Matthew 25:13)

78. The Mantle..168
   (2 Kings 2:14)

79. The Plan...170
   (Mark 11:2)

80. Abide...172
   (John 15:4)

81. Errrrbody...174
   (Acts 2:5, 14, 21)

82. Beyond Z...176
   (Genesis 12:1)

ACKNOWLEDGMENTS

Amy Cook, *Graphic Designer*
John Avis, *Proofreader*

The Pastor Search Committee:
Joe Livesay
Karen Smith
Amanda Gowen
Amy Moffatt
Tanya Mabry
Frank Huffman (deceased)
Andrew Smith

Foreword

The search committee knew that the candidate was young, but he came highly recommended. We were looking for either a young pastor who could relate to older people or an older pastor who could relate to young people.

When I first met Stephen Cook, I could not help but say to myself, "He really is young." At that time, I was 77 and he was 34 years old. I could have been his grandfather! I knew that I was on the committee to represent the interest of the older members of the church. When it came my turn to ask questions, I wanted to know which theologians had influenced his life. I was relived to hear names like Dietrich Bonhoeffer and Carlyle Marney.

The notes from my journal read, "We began to discuss subjects such as the mission of the church, the responsibilities of the pastor, the involvement of members in the kingdom of God, inclusion or exclusion of people with diverse backgrounds and beliefs, and ways to relate to different ages. His responses were thoughtful and well-reasoned. We then knew why his mentors had told us, 'He is mature beyond his age.'"

Soon after he came to Second Baptist Church, I felt a stirring in my pen. I have never wanted to outline or summarize the pastor's sermons, but many times something he said started my pen to writing. Later, after some reflection and thought, sometimes weeks or even months later, the scribbling was sorted out and organized and became what I call "Reflections."

Sometimes Stephen will say, "You said in nine lines what it took me 22 minutes to say." This little book contains "Reflections" from the first five years of Stephen Cook's ministry at Second Baptist Church, Memphis, Tennessee.

Andrew Smith

Preface

Shortly after I arrived in Memphis, I began to receive e-mails from an older man who had already endeared himself to my family during the pastoral search process. For quite a number of years—long before I began preaching—Andrew Smith has been listening intently from the back row of the choir loft. He listens with both his head and his heart. Then, as an act that can only be described as a rich spiritual discipline, he distills the preacher's message into concise reflections that capture the essence of the sermon. Many times I have said, "You put in a few lines what it took me 22 minutes to say."

Over almost five years I have been able to count on opening my inbox on Monday morning to receive these gifts he so graciously gives. As a preaching minister, I recognize that there are no other vocations that exist where people will, with every-seven-day-consistency, voluntarily give their time to listen to a single voice speaking for the time it takes to preach a sermon. That people are so deeply committed to that element of worship is a gift I do not take for granted.

But then to have a listener who takes the words that have been aimed at elucidating the Word and molds them into poetic reflections is a gift and an honor that is deeply humbling to me.

The reflections gathered here are rich and powerful expressions of a person who loves God with heart, soul, and mind. Andrew has put all three of those to work in assembling these writings. He has drawn the words in these pages from what has emerged after listening patiently, persistently for the Word of God proclaimed in my preaching.

Admittedly, when I began to receive Andrew's e-mails, I found them to be heartening. I have always been glad to receive them. It is nice to know that someone is listening. But when I read these lines now, assembled together in one collection, I am all the more honored. The collection sheds a light on my passion and ministry that no single sermon can provide.

I hope that, like me, you will find that Andrew's reflections will bring you closer to the One who is ever and always longing to be close to us. At the end of the day, our God is the one who is due all our expressions of worship.

Stephen Cook

Assurance

The Pause Button

*Then Peter said to Jesus, "Lord, it is good for us to be here;
if you wish, I will make three dwellings here,
one for you, one for Moses, and one for Elijah."*

Matthew 17:4

When Jesus, Peter, James, and John were visited by Moses and Elijah,
    Peter wanted to hit the pause button.

Jesus told Peter that regardless of how much he wanted to stay,
    they could not stay on the mountain.
There was work to be done.

Life moves only in the forward mode.
We do have a pause button, to think, to reflect,
But the realities of life must be lived as they occur.
It has neither a fast-forward nor a rewind button.

The task of salvation must move forward,
> even if the next mountain is called Calvary.

Jesus could not get to the resurrection without going to the cross.

We must not forget the glory of the transfiguration.
But we must move on to the task at hand.
The good news is that life is a journey that has both mountains and valleys.

Life does not, it *cannot*, remain the way it is.
Life moves on.
Jesus said, "I am with you."

Nowhere

The people murmured against Moses and said,
"Wherefore is this that thou hast brought us up out of Egypt?"
Exodus 17:3 (KJV)

WHAT DO YOU DO WHEN YOU FIND YOURSELF
    IN THE MIDDLE OF "NOWHERE"?

The journey may not be what you expected.
It may not be what you planned
    or even what you thought reasonable.

But that does not mean that God is not leading.
What you think the journey is about
    and where God is trying to lead you are not always
    the same.

You can find God in the most unexpected places.
You may be in the middle of "Nowhere,"
        but God specializes in "Nowhere."

If you are lost on your journey—rejoice!
Rejoice that you know you are lost
        and that God knows the way home.

It is when you turn to God and say, "What is next?"
        and realize that you are in the middle
        of "Nowhere"
        that God begins to lead you out.

Remember that God can always be found at "Nowhere,"
        and it is at "Nowhere"
        that God does his best work.

Rejoice!

Goodness and Mercy

*Surely goodness and mercy will follow me
all the days of my life.*

Psalm 23:6

GOODNESS AND MERCY ARE IN HOT PURSUIT!
THE HOUND OF HEAVEN IS NIPPING AT YOUR HEELS.

Move Christian—move!
Get on with your life.
Pick up the pace.
Get your motives right.
Search for your plan.
Find your purpose.
Pursue your magnum opus.

God is near.
He has always been near.
Make his plan your plan.

He will provide goodness and mercy,
> and you will dwell in the house of the Lord forever.

Green Pastures

He makes me lie down in green pastures.

Psalm 23:2

IT IS THE BARREN LAND BETWEEN PASTURES THAT PRESENTS THE DANGERS OF LIFE.
The valley of death is found in the transitions of life.

Life is a journey that goes through the deep and dark
      as well as along the high and bright highway.
The good news is that God is with us regardless of
where we are.

Life goes on.
The journey continues.
Even at the grave he is with us.

God, the good shepherd,
> leads us through all the days of our lives
> regardless of where the road may go.

Difficulties

See, the home of God is among mortals. He will dwell with them; they will be his peoples, and God himself will be with them; he will wipe every tear from their eyes.

Revelation 21:3-4

THERE HAVE ALWAYS BEEN DIFFICULTIES IN THIS WORLD:

      persecution,
      pestilence,
      intolerance,
      famine,
      war,
      and many other ways that humans deliver evil to each other.

History is laced with accounts of
> hardship,
> inequities,
> abuse,
> torture,
> pain,
> and it seems at times that we have learned very little.

Both Old and New Testaments are full of martyrs:
> Isaiah,
> Jeremiah,
> Peter,
> Paul,
> Jesus,
> and many others who gave their lives for their God.

History tells of saints in every age:
> Origen,
> Savonarola,
> Hus,
> Bunyan,
> Backus,
> men and women who stood tall in the face of evil.

At the great gathering at the throne of God
Everyone will stand shoulder to shoulder without rank.
The least in the Kingdom will stand beside the Bonhoeffers
and the Luthers and the Thressas and the Grahams.

Those who served in unnamed places,
Those whose efforts were not noticed by historians,
Those whose names have been lost in the mists of history,
Those who struggled with doubt as well as
Those who shouted from the housetops
Will all stand in equality because God loved them all with equal passion.

Transformed

*Be transformed by the renewing of your minds,
so that you may discern what is the will of God.*

Romans 12:2

IT IS NOT WHAT YOU ARE.
It is what God can make of you.

God calls you to be what you can be
    when you are sanctified by his Spirit.

What matters is what you are doing
    in the kingdom of God.

Remember, God does not give up on us
>   no matter what the circumstances of life may be.

Discover the deep gladness of surrendering
>   all to the will of God.

Even at the Grave

*You who fear the L*ORD*, praise him!... For he did not despise or abhor the affliction of the afflicted; he did not hide his face from me, but heard when I cried to him.*

Psalm 22:23-24

GOD ALWAYS TURNS TOWARD THOSE WHO ARE HURTING.
God is always active, moving toward need.

There is pain.
There is sorrow.
There is disappointment.
There is fear.
There is death.

There are losses that cannot be corrected.
There are times when life is shattered.

God cares as much for that which is broken
        as he cares for that which is whole.

Regardless of the damage,
        God is in the repair business.
He is the God who restores.

Even at the grave we can sing, "Alleluia!"

Remember

By this we know that we love the children of God, when we love God and obey his commandments.

1 John 5:2

Remember, God loves us because of who he is,
 not because of who we are.

Remember, God loves us with an unbelievable love,
 the gift of his son, Jesus Christ.

Remember, the heart of heaven has been given to us,
 but we cannot keep it—we must pass it on.

And

Remember, when we give it away,
        we cannot be selective.
It may go to some who are unworthy
        because in fact we are all unworthy.

Remember, it is not the result of giving;
        it is the fact of giving that matters.

Remember, you can never deplete the supply of God's love,
        no matter how much you give away.

You cannot out-give God.
He is a replenishing God!

Understanding

*When I look at your heavens, the work of your fingers,
the moon and the stars.*

Psalm 8:3

It is not difficult to understand the majesty of God:

    the stars,
    the sun,
    the moon,
    the universe!

It is so beyond us,
    so expansive,
    so magnificent!

What is difficult to understand is that
    love is boundless,
    grace is free,
    compassion is sure,
    truth is forever,
    understanding is absolute,
    forgiveness is complete,
    hope is vindicated.

God is real!
And miracles do happen!

To Strive

I press on toward the goal for the prize of the heavenly call of God in Christ Jesus.

Philippians 3:14

PAUL WAS DETERMINED TO PRESS,
    to follow the way of Christ,
    to strive.

Strive implies it is not easy.
Strive means there are questions.
Strive means it is a continuing struggle.

To *struggle* is to find the way to be one with Christ.
To *struggle* is to continue in the way of Christ.
To *struggle* is to support each other regardless.

The *way* is to accept God's grace.
The *way* is to live in God's love.
The *way* is to go forward together.

It is not whether or not God is on our side;
        it is whether or not we are on God's side.
"And if God is for us, who can be against us?"
                              (Romans 8:31)

Thanksgiving

But strive first for the kingdom of God and his righteousness, and all these things will be given to you as well.

Matthew 6:33

The Thanksgiving holiday was instituted by Abraham Lincoln in 1863
>on the occasion of the Battle of Antietam.

Thanks be to God, who is with us in the midst of
>tragedy,
>uncertainty,
>pain,
>and suffering.

We must be thankful for all of life:
> the joy and the pain,
> the good and the bad,
> the beautiful and the ugly.

Remember that God knows.
Jesus suffered.
He was rejected.
He died.
But then there was Easter!
God understands, and he knows how to restore.

Life is not perfect.
Everything is not okay all the time,
> but the word "restore" is real.
Be thankful for a God who restores!

The Same Mind

Let the same mind be in you that was in Christ Jesus.

Philippians 2:5

LET THIS MIND BE IN YOU, WHICH WAS IN CHRIST JESUS:
- humble,
- obedient,
- loving,
- serving,
- sacrificing.

That is so different than the mind in most of us:
> greedy,
> arrogant,
> defiant,
> selfish,
> proud.

What if we could have a mind like the mind in Christ Jesus?
> love as he loved!
> serve as he served!
> obey as he obeyed!
> sacrifice as he sacrificed!
> die as he died!

But!

He arose!
The cross was not the end;
> the cross was the beginning!

In All Things

Give thanks in all circumstances.

1 Thessalonians 5:18

Give thanks *IN* all,
 not *for* all.

> Sing praises to the Lord, O you his faithful ones, and give thanks to his holy name. For his anger is but for a moment; his favor is for a lifetime. Weeping may linger for the night, but joy comes in the morning.
> (Psalm 30:4-5)

Give thanks for a God who will not give up on us
> regardless of the circumstances,
> regardless of anything life can deliver,
> regardless of joy and pain and sorrow.

Give thanks in all things.

Courage

One day Peter and John were going up to the temple at the hour of prayer.... And a man lame from birth was being carried in. When he saw Peter and John about to go into the temple, he asked them for alms. Peter looked intently at him, as did John, and said, "Look at us."

Acts 3:1-4

WHEN PETER AND JOHN WENT TO THREE O'CLOCK PRAYERS,
> the lame man was there.
There was no avoiding him.

Luke carefully tells about the perceptions:
> When Peter saw the lame man,
> He said, "Look at us."

Perception is everything.

Robert Frost said,
> "How many things have to happen to you before something occurs to you?"

What happened was Pentecost!
After Pentecost everything was different!

The courage
> to look,
> to see,
> to feel,
> to care,
> to touch,
> to do what needs to be done.

That takes courage.

It takes courage to face the uncertainties of life.
It takes courage to face pain and suffering.

But when courage is in action,
> church happens.

Circumstances

But the LORD was with Joseph and showed him steadfast love.

Genesis 39:21

JOSEPH WAS THE COVENANT RECIPIENT OF GOD'S LOVE,

    but that did not guarantee an easy, trouble-free life.

There is a big difference between the dreams we dream and the reality we get.
That does not mean we can give up the struggle.
We cannot stop dreaming.
The reality of life is many times not fair; it is not right.

It is not only interracial riots in other cities.
It is not only religious conflict in the Middle East
It is not only the outbreak of a deadly virus in Africa.

We all have setbacks.
We all have disappointments,
We all have failures.

The Lord always loved Joseph.
Regardless of his circumstances,
       the Lord was with Joseph.

And the good news is that the Lord is with us.
God's promise is "I will be with you"
       (Matthew 28:20)
       regardless of the circumstances of life.

The Devil and the Deep Red Sea

*The LORD went in front of them in a pillar of cloud by day...
and in a pillar of fire by night.... The Egyptians pursued
them...and overtook them camped by the sea.... But Moses
said to the people, "Do not be afraid, stand firm, and see the
deliverance that the LORD will accomplish.*

Exodus 13:21; 14:9, 13

THE CHILDREN OF ISRAEL WERE HAPPY WITH THEIR DELIVERANCE
    until they found themselves trapped
    between the devil and the deep Red Sea.

Life can sometimes be a trap between two bad options,
    but the way forward must start in the trap,
    and the Lord knows the way out.

Whatever the crisis may be in our own lives,
> we must remember that the Lord will fight for us.

His promises are true regardless of what the situation may be.

It is not easy to "be still and wait upon the Lord."
> (Exodus 14:13)

That means we must give up control,
> which might put us in an unexpected place.

We might very well be *between the devil and the deep Red Sea*,
> and we may have no option but to *be still and wait upon the Lord.*

But do not be surprised at what the Lord can do.

Face to Face

What we do know is this: when he is revealed, we will be like him, for we will see him as he is.

1 John 3:2

When you come to a fork in the road, take it.

Yogi Berra

IN TIME WE WILL TAKE THAT ULTIMATE FORK IN THE ROAD,
      but death will not win because we will then see Jesus.

We are double blessed because we also see him now
      in the face of all those who keep the faith
      regardless of circumstances,
      regardless of sorrow,
      regardless of grief.

Those who keep the faith in the midst of devastating illnesses like
>cancer,
>Alzheimer's,
>Parkinson's,
>or simply old age.

Jesus is in the neighborhood.
We see him in the love manifested by our friends.
So let us choose to love today, regardless,
>and thereby be a part of that great army of those who mirror the face of Jesus.

>*And I shall see him face to face and tell the story,*
>*saved by grace.*
>(Fanny Crosby)

Reality

And Jesus said to them, "Follow me and I will make you fish for people."

Mark 1:17

IT IS NOT WHAT YOU PLAN TO DO.
It is what you are given to do.

Sometimes you do not choose your mission.
Sometimes your mission chooses you.

Be alert!
Listen!
Look!

What is it out there?
What do you do about it?

It is not how you plan to deal with the uncertainties of life.
It is how you deal with the uncertainties of life.

Face reality.
Fight demons that get in your way.

Remember.

You are not alone.
Launch out in faith.
Go forth in the Spirit.
Do what needs to be done.

"Lo, I am with you always."
   (Matthew 28:20)

Love... Hope... Joy

Joseph and God

Her husband Joseph, being a righteous man and unwilling to expose her to public disgrace, planned to dismiss her quietly.... An angel of the Lord appeared to him in a dream, and said, "Joseph, son of David, do not be afraid to take Mary as your wife, for the child conceived in her is from the Holy Spirit."... He did as the angel of the Lord commanded him; he took her as his wife, but had no marital relations with her until she had borne a son; and he named him Jesus.

Matthew 1:19-20, 24-25

What the love of a man can do…
>Divorce her quietly.
>Dismiss her privately.
>
>Do it with love and kindness.
>Do it with as little publicity as possible.

What the love of God can do…
>The angel—
>The angel changed everything!
>
>The change was radical.
>The change was unbelievable.

What the love of God and the love of a man can do…
>Joseph did as the angel said.
>And he said nothing!
>
>Joseph, the silent man in Scripture.
>The silent man became God's enabler!

What the love of God and the love of Christians can do today…
>If we listen for God's message,
>>if we have the courage to be obedient,
>
>We can be like Joseph.
>We can be God's enabler.

Blessed

*Great crowds followed him.... When Jesus saw the crowds,
he went up the mountain; and after he sat down his disciples
came to him. Then he began to speak, and taught them.*

Matthew 4:25–5:2

HE TAUGHT THE CROWD:
    the hurting,
    the depressed,
    the lonely,
    the anxious,
    the worried,
    the guilty.

He did not say, "Blessed are…"
> the wealthy,
> the successful,
> the healthy,
> the educated,
> the influential,
> the powerful,
> the elite.

He said, "Blessed are…"
> the poor,
> the mourners,
> the meek,
> the merciful,
> the pure in heart,
> the peacemakers,
> the persecuted.

Illogical words,
Irrational words,
Impractical words, but…

Blessed are those who don't have it together.
Blessed are those who are real, ordinary people.
Blessed are those who hunger and thirst after righteousness.

Blessed are those who want to do the real thing in God's real world,
> a world that is hurting and in desperate need of the love of God.

Salt

*You are the salt of the earth: but if the salt has lost its taste,
how can its saltiness be restored?*

Matthew 5:13

YOU MAY BE ORDINARY, COMMON PEOPLE LIKE THE CROWD JESUS TALKED TO ON THE MOUNT.
But that does not mean you are not important.

Or

You may even be one of those who wants to cause a commotion,
> stir up trouble,
>> or start a revolution.

But

If you are a Christian,
> you are in the salting business,
> the changing business,
> the enhancing business.

The church is a "no audition—no cut" organization.
There are no rejects in God's kingdom.

Jesus did not say you are *like* salt
> or that you *can* be salt
> or that you *might* be salt
> or that you *should* be salt.

He said you *are* the salt of the earth.

The question is:
Do you still taste like salt, or are you tasteless?

Whatever the love of God is,
> you are the embodiment of it.

The Fight

But I say to you that if you are angry with a brother or sister, you will be liable to judgment.

Matthew 5:22

We are all familiar with jokes that end with the line
"And that is when the fight started."

Jesus had a lot to say about conflict in the human family.

If we are serious about the business of being a Christian,
    we do not get to choose who we love.
The Word of God living and being in us
    changes the way we relate to others.

When there is something wrong in the human family,
    we must take the initiative to make it right.
It does not matter whether or not we are successful.
What matters is that we do everything we know to do to
resolve the matter.

Regardless of who started the fight,
    the person of God is responsible for trying to make
    it right.

It is not that we are angry.
There are things that should make us angry.
It is that we cannot let anger consume us.
We cannot let anger control our lives.

In order to make peace with your enemy,
    you must first make peace with yourself.

If we are to live the life God wants us to live,
    we must give ourselves to the task of making right
    what has gone wrong in our human family.

Choose

The LORD God took the man and put him in the garden of Eden to till it and keep it.... When the woman saw that the tree was good for food...she took of its fruit and ate.... The LORD God sent him forth from the garden of Eden.

Genesis 2:15; 3:6, 23

THE GATES CLOSED.

And ever since we have been striving to be what we cannot be.
We cannot be like God.

But

We can be what God intended us to be.
We can work and take care of the earth.

We can choose to do the work God gave us to do.
We can choose how we are going to do that work.

Every day we can choose to love God.
Every day we can choose to live the life we have been given.

We cannot reopen the gates,
    but we can choose
        life,
        love,
        peace,
        and joy.

A Living Hope

Blessed be the God and father of our Lord Jesus Christ!
By his great mercy he has given us a new birth into a living
hope through the resurrection of Jesus Christ from the dead.

1 Peter 1:3

THE GOOD NEWS IS THAT CHRIST HAS BEEN RAISED FROM THE DEAD.
But life is not always lived in the colors and hues of Easter.
The new revelation of God brought to us by Christ Jesus
raised as many questions as it brought answers.

How does this new revelation of God deal with the realities of life?
Storms and earthquakes?
Tsunamis and sickness?
Pain and tragedies of all kinds?

Where is the strength and power required to deal with
life today?
In the bottom of every heart, there is a little pool of tears.
There is uncertainty.
There is doubt and pain.

Peter's message to the early church was that there is hope.
God never promised ease and comfort,
> but he did promise that we will never be forced
> to face the trials of life alone.

Jesus experienced all the demands of life.
He understands pain.
He understands disappointment.
He understands death.

By the mercies of God, there is hope.
There may or may not be healing.
There may or may not be release from pain.
There may or may not be understanding.

But you do not walk alone.
Even Jesus died.
Even Jesus experienced pain.
Even Jesus cried, "My God, my God, why have you forsaken me?" (Matthew 27:46)

You do not walk alone.
Jesus lives, and he loves you even now.

Leave!

I go to prepare a place for you.

John 14:2

Go?
As in leave?
What do you mean "leave"?
No way!
Not yet!

"Let not your hearts be troubled."
(John 14:27)

That is asking too much.
Of course we are troubled.

Just give us specific directions.
We don't know what is going on.
All we see is trouble.

You do not need specifics.
All you need is to believe in me.
God is in me and is closer than you can imagine.

God loves you.
His love is the good news.
Let his love flow through you.

Take the love I have given you, and share it with others.
Be a bearer of the truth, and God will be with you.
God is alive and moving with power within you.

Do not be afraid.
Ask anything in my name.
Be the love of God to those who need you.

Weeds

The kingdom of heaven may be compared to someone who sowed good seed in his field; but while everybody was asleep, an enemy came and sowed weeds among the wheat.

Matthew 13:24-25

A weed is simply a plant whose virtues have not yet been discovered.

Ralph Waldo Emerson

THE GOSPEL IS FULL OF SURPRISES.
Those on the inside are on the outside.
Those on the outside are on the inside.

You can't tell the difference by simply looking at it.

We are not responsible for deciding who are weeds and who
are valuable plants.
God loves them all.
God is the judge.

The kingdom of God is open to all.
Do not limit the love of God.

Our job is to be the presence of God in the whole world.
Scatter the seed everywhere.
Throw it on every person.

You do not know what the love of God can do!

Fair

So the last will be first, and the first will be last.

Matthew 20:16

GOD'S GRACE IS NOT A MATTER OF BEING FAIR.
Grace does not pretend to be fair.
It is deliberately unfair.

It is outrageous.
It is ostentatious.
It is given to everyone.

Regardless.
Regardless of anything.
Regardless of everything.

We cannot begrudge God because he is gracious.
We can only rejoice that we are recipients of his grace.
The economy of the kingdom of God is grace—
pure and simple.

We are all late in the game.
Grace has nothing to do with our merit,
        who we are or what we are.

It has everything to do with God's love
        and his determination to give grace to everyone.
Thanks be to God that God is not fair.

The Table
World Communion Sunday

There is one body and one Spirit, just as you were called to the one hope of your calling, one Lord, one faith, one baptism, one God and Father of all, who is above all and through all and in all.

Ephesians 4:4-6

As the Apostle Paul said,
 "Nothing can separate us from the love of God."
                              (Romans 5:39)

We have a difficult time remembering just how big the table of the Lord is.
The table is big enough for every one of us.

Remember, "God so loved the world that he gave his
only Son" (John 3:16)
For us!

Remember that they (the least of these) are loved just as much
as anyone else
  and that they are just as welcome at God's table as
  any of us.

Pray that God will help us bridge the gap between our
selfishness
  and the vastness of his love.

Where Is the Joy?

*He was transfigured before them.... Then Peter said,
"Let us make three dwellings."*

Mark 9:2, 5

THE TRANSFIGURATION WAS THE PIVOT POINT
IN THE MINISTRY OF JESUS.
But Peter did not want to change; he wanted to stay.
He wanted to build a shelter and prolong the present.

But God—God is of the future.

Mountaintops are great
      but only if they are a launching place toward
      the future.

We can find excitement and a thrill on top of the mountain,
> but it is in the valley that we find joy.

Joy comes from doing what must be done.
Joy comes from investing your life in the will of God.
Joy comes from
> moving on,
> taking risks,
> exposing yourself to pain,
> loving without expectation of reward,
> doing God's work,
> fighting evil,
> doing battle with Satan,
> healing the sick,
> making sinners whole,
> lifting up the downtrodden,
> reaching out to the needy.
> being the hands of Jesus in a needy world.

That is where you find joy.

Wonder

The heavens are telling the glory of God; and the firmament proclaims his handiwork.

Psalm 19:1

How can we see the wonder of God's creation through all this stuff?

How can we see his magnificence when we are consumed by the mundane?

How can we see his glory when we are numb from the bombardments of life?

But—
When we consider the mystery and magnificence and wonder
of God's creation,
When we consider the mystery and magnificence and wonder
of God's infinite love,
> we realize that the closer we get to God,
> the more questions we have
> and that the closer we get to God, the larger God
> gets and the smaller we get.

But—
That is when the miracle happens!
That is when we realize that God really is close
> and his arms are embracing us in his everlasting love.

Praise God from whom all blessings flow.

Declare the Word

I treasure your word in my heart, so that I may not sin against you. Blessed are you, O LORD; teach me your statutes. With my lips I declare all the ordinances of your mouth.

Psalm 119:11-13

How do we guard the Word of God and hand off the good news to the world?

It is not easy.
First we have to decide which Word we are talking about.
There are many differences of opinion about the Word.
How do we deal with all the conflicts in the church?

The bottom line is that the Bible tells us about Jesus,
    and Jesus shows us the way to God the Father.

Even in the Psalms there was a continuing search for the living Word.

Be open to the living Word, and let that Word influence your life.

Let there be an infusion of grace, compassion, and love.

Hosanna!

Then those who went ahead and those who followed were shouting, "Hosanna!"

Mark 11:9

REMEMBER THAT HOSANNA MEANS "SAVE US."
God had saved them before,
       and they wanted him to do it again.

Is this the time?
Is this the leader?
Is this the Messiah?

They may not have known exactly who he was,
> but if he could save them, they didn't care.

Jesus knew they were filled with false hope,
> but he was there to show God's love—regardless.

The burden of love is loving,
> and that is exactly what he did.

It was not required that they understand.

There would be time for understanding later—
> after the cross,
> after the resurrection,
> after Pentecost.

Then they understood—some of them—
> and that is all that was necessary.

In time the love of God will do its work.

> "God so loved the world that he gave his only Son."
> (John 3:16)

Gifts

Now there are varieties of gifts, but the same Spirit.

1 Corinthians 12:4

THE QUESTION IS NOT WHETHER OR NOT YOU ARE A MINISTER.

The question is "What kind of a minister are you?"

The question is "What gifts do you bring to the altar,
    and what gifts do you take away from the altar to
    give away to others?"

The question is not "Who is worthy?"
In truth none of us is worthy,
        but we are all recipients of God's grace.
The question is "Do we keep our gifts, or do we give them away?"

Give thanks for God's gifts!
Give God's gifts to others.

That Woman

A Samaritan woman came to draw water.

John 4:7

WHO WAS THAT WOMAN?
Who knows?
Her past is irrelevant to the story.
She had a past—we all have a past—
     but it is what we do with the present that counts.

She took her newfound news and told everybody.
She was the first person in the New Testament to declare that "the Christ has come."
She talked with Jesus.
Jesus talked with her.

If he would talk with that woman, whom else might he talk with?
Does the fact that he talked with that woman
> mean that we are expected to talk with people like that?

Nowhere in the record is God limited by our prejudices.
What we believe does not limit God.

God so loved the world.
How much do we love?

Limits

They were saying, "Is not this Jesus, the son of Joseph?"

John 6:42

THE JEWS WERE NOT SO MUCH ASTOUNDED BY WHAT HE SAID BUT BY WHO HE WAS!

He did not fit the bill.
He was nothing close to what they expected.

When we limit our world to what we know or perceive,
    we can miss God's grace.
We limit God's power by filtering it through our own knowledge.

"Anyone who comes to me, I will never drive away."
Anyone?   (John 6:37)

How, then, can we set limits?
How can we confine the love of God to what we know?
Did he not say, "God so loved the world?"
                              (John 3:16)

"Open my eyes, that I may see glimpses of truth thou hast for me." (Clara H. Scott)

Mindset

But to set the mind on the Spirit is life and peace.

Romans 8:6

SET YOUR MIND ON THE SPIRIT.
Break loose from the here and now.
Focus on what God is doing.
Look for where God is at work.
Be mindful of the power of God.
Search for a deeper awareness of God in action.
Set your mind on what God's mind is set on.

You might be surprised by what happens.
You might change your attitude.
You might love the unlovely.
You might even be Christian!

The Made-up Mind

Surely the Messiah does not come from Galilee, does he?...
No prophet is to arise from Galilee.

John 7:41, 52

DOES HE?
Does the Messiah come out of Galilee?
No way!

How dangerous can a made-up mind be?
Is it possible that we do not know everything?
Have we established boundaries that are absolutely rigid?
Does it matter what the evidence is?

What is the cost of expanding your boundaries?
How far can you let your compassion go?

Some of us asked the question:
Who ever wanted to go to Memphis?
Is it possible that God wants us to live and love in Memphis?
"Wherever he leads, I'll go" does not always mean some faraway place.

Lord, help us love our neighbor.

> "Love the Lord your God, and your neighbor
> as yourself." (Luke 10:27)

That's a little radical, don't you think?

Hope and Suffering

Through whom we have obtained access to this grace in which we stand; and we boast in our hope of sharing the glory of God.

Romans 5:2

THE PATHWAY FROM SUFFERING TO HOPE IS NOT A STRAIGHT LINE.
Sometimes the best we can get is a strange mixture of suffering and hope.
And when you get to hope, you do not necessarily leave suffering behind.

Hope in the midst of suffering is a most precious commodity.

"And hope does not disappoint us." (Romans 5:5)

Hope does not erase suffering,
but hope can make suffering meaningful.

The Choice

Choose this day whom you will serve...but as for me and my household, we will serve the LORD.

Joshua 24:15

WHEN TIMES ARE GOOD, IT IS EASY TO CHOOSE TO SERVE THE LORD,
but things do not always turn out as we expect them to.

We fully intend to do what is right,
      but, alas, we are human.

The fact is that we have to choose over and over again which God we are going to serve. Are we going to give our loyalty to God or not?

The significant thing is that whether we are loyal or not, God remains the same.
It was God
> who called,
> who led,
> who sustained,
> who rescued,
> who was always faithful regardless of what the choices were.

The children of Israel
> wavered,
> disobeyed,
> abandoned their faith,
> forgot about their God.

But God never changed.
God always remained faithful.

Choose you this day, and every day, the God you will serve.
We get to choose every day whether or not we will serve the Lord,
> but regardless of what we do, God loves us
> without condition.

That, my friend, is good news.
Praise the Lord!

The Light

Jesus answered them, "The hour has come."

John 12:23

To live life in the light of death is something altogether different from living life in the shadow of death.

Chuck Poole

WHEN IT IS TIME TO DIE, IT IS TIME TO DIE.

The question is, "How do we use the time?"
We can choose to live in the light,
      or we can choose to live in the shadow.

Life in the light is active;
      it is positive;
      it is progressive.

Use the light to illuminate your path.
Use the light to illuminate the path of others.

Value your life while you live it,
> because whether the light goes out instantly like
a switch
or whether it goes out like a slowly turned dimmer,
when it is out, it is out.

Remember, when life is lived in the light of Christ,
> the end is not darkness.

The end is light.

Because

So they went out and fled from the tomb, for terror and amazement had seized them; and they said nothing to anyone, for they were afraid.

Mark 16:8

Some of the oldest manuscripts of Mark 16:8 end with a word that can be translated "because."

Stephen Cook

BECAUSE...
Because?
Because!

He is alive!
He is not here.
Things have changed.

So...
So what?
So what now?

It is not over.
It is a new beginning.
It is the beginning of the good news.

Good news—Jesus has risen.
Good news—death does not win.
Good news—Christ the Lord is risen today!

Challenge

Get Ready

*In those days John the Baptist appeared
in the wilderness of Judea, proclaiming, "
Repent, for the kingdom of heaven has come near."*

Matthew 3:1-2

John the Baptist was not a gentle man!

Stephen Cook

John steps out on center stage and says,
"Get Ready!"
Repent!
For the day of the Lord is at hand.

Get prepared!
Pay attention!
Focus on what is important!

Get ready for the surprise of all surprises.
The Messiah is here.
Don't miss him.
Behold the Lamb of God!

What are you going to do about it?
What are we going to do about it?

It is no less important now than it was then.
You can only react to the message of God in the time and place you have been given.

What do you say?
What do you do?

Darkness and Light

Arise, shine; for your light has come, and the glory of the LORD is risen upon you.

Isaiah 60:1

THE LIGHT HAS COME, BUT THERE IS STILL DARKNESS. The good news is that the darkness can never put out the light.

The question is "What can we do to reduce the darkness?" Regardless of how dark circumstances may be, our light can shine.

Whatever life brings, we must live it.
Can we live it with confidence?
Can we live it with grace?
Can we live it with joy?

The darkness is not going to win.
God always shows up where it is the darkest.

Don't wait!
Get with it!
Our light has come!
Now is the day for action!

> "You are a chosen race, a royal priesthood,
> a holy nation, God's own people, in order that you
> may proclaim the mighty acts of him who called you
> out of darkness into his marvelous light."
> (1 Peter 2:9)

Darkness cannot drive out darkness; only light can do that. Hate cannot drive out hate; only love can do that.
Martin Luther King Jr.

Worry

So do not worry about tomorrow, for tomorrow will bring worries of its own.

Matthew 6:34

Do not worry!
He has got to be kidding!
If you care at all,
      you worry.

He is talking about *stuff!*
Security.
Comfort.
Protection.
Stuff and more stuff!

Be careful where you place your focus.
You cannot focus on God and stuff.
Jesus did not preach a prosperity gospel.
Jesus said that you must be the giver, not the consumer.

It is not a matter of whether or not you will choose.
It is a matter of which way of life you choose.

You cannot choose both God and stuff.
Keep your stuff, and worry about it.
Give up your stuff, and give up worry.

Bones

Then he said to me, "Prophesy to these bones and say to them, 'O dry bones, hear the word of the LORD!'"

Ezekiel 37:4

IT IS ONE THING TO LIVE,
> but it is another thing to be ALIVE.

We live,
> but are we alive?

Ezekiel's dry bones came alive when God's prophet spoke.
It was not whether or not God could or could not make the bones come alive.
It was whether or not the prophet had the vision and the courage to prophesy.

The question is "Do we have the vision and courage to prophesy?"
The good news is that God can still cause change.
Dry bones can rise and walk again.

Do it!
Speak!
Prophesy!

Do it!
Speak!
Prophesy!

Rise up, and praise the Lord!

Who Is Not My Neighbor?

And who is my neighbor?

Luke 10:29

If the question was valid when it was asked of Jesus,
> it is certainly valid in this day of instant communication.

Perhaps the question should be "Who is *not* my neighbor?"

Even though we quickly quote John 3:16—
> "God so loved the world that he gave his only Son"—
> we struggle with the question.

What about the Taliban?
What about Al-Qaeda?
What about Iranians, the North Koreans?

Have those of us with gray hair forgotten about those so-called...
    "Sneaky, dirty little Japs"?
    "Arrogant, evil Germans"?
    "Greasy, smelly Italians"?*

We all have a problem with accepting the message that everyone is a neighbor
    and that Jesus died for everyone.

Jesus said, "Go and do likewise."
Go and love your neighbor.

---

*The propaganda of the 1940s made bigots of all of us who lived during World War II.

Touched

*A leper came to him begging him, and kneeling he said to him,
"If you choose, you can make me clean."
Moved with pity, Jesus stretched out his hand
and touched him.*

Mark 1:40-41

*The word translated "pity" is in common English
more like "incensed" or even "anger."*

Stephen Cook

We can speculate as to why he was upset.
Was it because the leper implied that he might not *choose* to give healing?
Was it because of the social system that excluded people with leprosy?
Was it because lepers were untouchable?

When Jesus touched him, he broke the Law.
He did not have to touch him to heal him.
He had healed others without touching them.

What does that teach us?
Are there rules we should break to extend love and healing to our fellow man?

Jesus broke the Law of Moses to heal the leper,
> and the leper broke the command of Jesus to not tell what had happened.

He told everybody!

God help us to be radical proclaimers of the love of Jesus.

Wilderness Time

And the Spirit immediately drove him out into the wilderness.

Mark 1:12

*He was **driven** into the wilderness.*

Stephen Cook

Time for testing.
Time for reflection.
Time for preparation.
Time for leaving the past.
Time for moving forward.

Devoid of routine.
Stripped of comfort.
Empty of human support.
Separated from companions.
Reduced to utter dependence.

Ready to do the work of the kingdom.
Prepared for an infilling of the Holy Spirit.

Lord, drive us into the wilderness.
Prepare us for our work in your kingdom.

The Lame Man

Now when they saw the boldness of Peter and John and realized that they were uneducated men, they were amazed.

Acts 4:13

WHY DOES SOMETHING LIKE HEALING A LAME MAN CAUSE SO MUCH TROUBLE?
Why was everyone so upset because a lame man could finally walk?

What was the difference in the healing Peter and the Peter warming by the fire?
Where did the defiant Peter before the Sanhedrin come from?
Where did Peter get the power to heal the lame man?

Could it be that the Holy Spirit made a courageous man out of a coward?
Could it be that the Holy Spirit can make a radical change in us?

Grant us the humility to surrender to the spirit of God.
Spirit, fill us!
Spirit, change us!

Horror of Horrors

*But when they believed Philip, ...they were baptized,
both men and women.*

Acts 8:12

*Philip was causing trouble in the church!
He was out of bounds!*

Stephen Cook

PHILIP WAS NOT ONLY PREACHING TO THE SAMARITANS.
They accepted the gospel, and horror of horrors,
Philip baptized them!

Regardless of what the Christians in Jerusalem thought,
God had no respect for the wall they had built—
No matter how high and how secure they thought it was.

They sent Peter and John to straighten things out.
But horror of horrors when they laid hands on the Samaritans,
The Spirit came upon them.

The good news is that the spirit of God has descended upon us—
No matter how formal and ritualistic we might be.
God has work for us to do, and the Spirit will empower us
to do it.

Let the Spirit move.
Be open to new power.
Get ready for the Spirit.
The spirit of God wants to live in you and empower you to do
a new and wonderful ministry in the kingdom of God.

Are you open?
Are you willing?
Are you ready?

There is no limit to the power of the Holy Spirit.
Horror of horrors, your life might be radically changed!

Success

And they said to him, "Grant us to sit, one at your right hand and one at your left, in your glory."

Mark 10:37

WHAT WAS WRONG WITH BEING AMBITIOUS?
Why should James and John not want success?
Why should they not strive to be the best?

The question is—ambitious for what?
The question is—what kind of success?
The question is—what is the cost of being the best?

The bottom line for James and John was
    "Do you really know what you are asking for?"

The bottom line for us is
> "Do we really want the sacrifice that service demands?"

Using Sight

*Bartimaeus son of Timaeus, a blind beggar,
was sitting by the roadside. When he heard that it was
Jesus of Nazareth, he began to shout out and say,
"Jesus, Son of David, have mercy on me!"
Many sternly ordered him to be quiet,
but he cried out even more loudly.... Jesus stood still
and said, "Call him here."... Then Jesus said to him,
"What do you want me to do for you?"
The blind man said to him, "My teacher, let me see again."
Jesus said to him, "Go; your faith has made you well."
Immediately he regained his sight
and followed him on the way.*

Mark 10:46-49, 51-52

We know what blind Bartimaeus wanted.
He wanted to see.
He wanted the freedom that sight would give him.

We know what Jesus wanted.
He wanted to heal.
He wanted to demonstrate the power of God.

But what did the others want?
Why did they urge Bartimaeus to be quiet?
Why did they want the blind man to hold his peace?

Jesus asked Bartimaeus,
    "What do you want me to do for you?"

Bartimaeus wanted to see,
    and he used his sight to follow Jesus.

Jesus is asking us,
    "What do you want from me?"

Do we really want to see Jesus?
Are we ready to follow like Bartimaeus?

Gathered

Let the nations gather together, and let the peoples assemble.

Isaiah 43:9

It mattered to Isaiah that the people show up.
The people needed to be connected.
They needed to remember who they were.

In the twenty-first century we are the most connected people in all of history:
E-mail, Facebook, Twitter, LinkedIn, and new social media being invented every day.
The problem today is not connection.
The problem is privacy.

There is now a Virtual Online Church!
> No requirements.
> No rules.
> No obligations.
> No records.
> No connections.
> (Just send your money.)

The truth is that God does make demands.
Grace is free, but response is required.
Serving God is a challenge.
We are challenged to do something.

We are a gathering people because in church, together,
we worship God and gain the strength to share God's
grace and mercy with others.

If we can do it "in church,"
> we might be able to do it out there in the world where
> ministry is needed.

We are gathered
> with all our diversity,
> with all our differences,
> with all our varied history,
> with all our talents.

And when we mix it all together,
> we have a stronger message than any of us can
> proclaim on our own.

Yes, But...

Then I said, "Ah, Lord GOD! Truly I do not know how to speak, for I am only a boy." But the LORD said to me, "Do not say, 'I am only a boy';... Do not be afraid of them, for I am with you."

Jeremiah 1:6-7, 8

MOST OF US LIVE THE GIVEN LIFE, NOT THE PLANNED LIFE.

In the process of living, God shows up and life changes.

It is the changes in life that present the problem.
    "Yes, but..."
It is the "but" events that shape us and determine who we are.

The Bible is full of "Yes, but…" stories.
> Moses,
> Samuel,
> Jeremiah,
> Isaiah,
> Amos,
> Jonah,
> Paul.

Remember, the message of God is "Fear not."
I would not call you if I could not give you the strength you need.

We are all called to be ministers of the gospel,
> called to glorify the name of God,
> called to share the good news,
> called to be instruments of God's grace,
> regardless of circumstances,
> regardless of excuses,
> regardless of "Yes, but…"

We are in the business of making disciples in and for the kingdom of God.

Mary's Perfume

Mary took a pound of costly perfume made of pure nard, anointed Jesus' feet, and wiped them with her hair.

John 12:3

WHERE DID MARY GET ENOUGH MONEY TO BUY THAT MUCH PERFUME?
What was she planning to do with it?

She did not use it when her brother died.
She was not married.
She had no children.
She had a conflict with her sister.

Was she saving it for herself?
Her wedding?
Her burial?

The question is not how you get your resources.
For some people it is inherited.
For some people it is given.
For some people it is earned.
For some people it is generous.
For some people it is meager.

It is how you use your resources that matters.
Do you use it to serve the Master?
Do you use it to serve others?

Tags

*Those who had seen him before as a beggar began to ask,
"Is this not the man who used to sit and beg?"*

John 9:8

Everyone has a tag.

Stephen Cook

The man was "tagged" as the blind beggar.

Beware of the tag you put on people.

Remember, you have a tag too.
>"Old guy."
>"Young kid."
>"Conservative."
>"Liberal."
>"Do-gooder."
>"Skinflint."

You cannot see the other person until you remove their tag.
Open my eyes that I might see the miracles you have made
>in me,
>in others,
>in the church!

Imitators

Therefore be imitators of God, as beloved children, and walk in love, as Christ loved us.

Ephesians 5:1-2

Imitate God! That is a tall order!

Stephen Cook

How do we do that?
How do we even try?

First, look at what Jesus did.

How did he pray?
When did he pray?
What did he pray?

What was his attitude?
Who did he minister to?
How did he minister?

If we want to imitate God,
      we may have to widen our circle.
We may have to reach out to the unlovely.

To imitate God,
      that is a tall order!

Unique

David strapped Saul's sword over the armor, and he tried in vain to walk, for he was not used to them. Then David said to Saul, "I cannot go with these, for I have not tested them."

1 Samuel 17:39

We all see ourselves as the "little guy."
We all pull for the little guy David.
Nobody wants the big guy, Goliath, to win.

On the other hand,
    we want to be the big guy,
        strong, well equipped, ready to fight.

David said Goliath was so big he could not miss him.
But David could not be who he was in Saul's armor.
He could not do what had to be done if he was not who he was.

The church cannot be what it is not.
This church must be what it is.
We may admire the success of other churches,
        but we must not copy them.

We may be "Second Baptist,"
        but we are second to none
           if we are what we are called to be.

We must be a unique church
        with a unique message
        that ministers in a unique way
        to those who need us.

Called

From there he moved on to the hill country on the east of Bethel, and pitched his tent.... And there he built an altar to the LORD and invoked the name of the LORD.

Genesis 12:8

WHEN ABRAM AND SARAI REACHED THE LAND OF CANAAN,
They built an altar everywhere they stopped.
They honored each place with prayer and worship.
They centered their lives on faith and dedication.

Then, and only then, they moved
       into the future,
       into the unknown,
       into a life of service.

You have to listen to hear the call.
You have to prepare yourself with prayer to have the courage
to move into a life of service.
You have to let your heart be molded in tenderness to love
the unlovely.

We have all come from somewhere,
       and we are all going somewhere,
           but it is now, right here, that we must remember
           God's gift of love and our calling to love others.

       This is the day that the Lord has made; let us rejoice and
       be glad in it.
       (Psalm 118:24)

Let us use this day for the advancement of the kingdom of God.

Afraid!

The angel said to her, "Do not be afraid, Mary, for you have found favor with God."

Luke 1:30

Any normal person would be afraid.

Stephen Cook

EVERY TIME AN ANGEL SHOWS UP, FEAR COMES WITH HIM.

Angels are not needed for common events.

How many questions do you think flashed through her mind?
    I'm just a girl.
    I'm not married.
    I'm still a virgin.

What about Joseph?
What about my family?
What about my neighbors?

Are you sure?
You've got to be kidding.
This is not what I had planned.

At least those are the questions we would have asked.
Are we open to the possibility that an angel might be speaking to us?
What is he asking us to do?
Are we willing to let him disrupt our lives?

Can we say with Mary, "Let it be with me"?

New Truth

*Then he said, "Into what then were you baptized?"
They answered, "Into John's baptism."*

Acts 19:3

All of the truth that you know is not all of the truth.

Stephen Cook

BE ALERT.
Be open.
Be willing to learn new truth.

> "Jesus answered, 'I saw you under the fig tree before Philip called you.' Nathanael replied, 'Rabbi, you are the Son of God.'"
> (John 1:48-49)

Everything you can see is not everything to be seen.

Start now, with what you can see, and wait for the future
to unfold.

And when it is revealed, do what needs to be done then.
And when that is done, do what is revealed to you next.

It is the unfolding of life that makes it vital and meaningful.
Sit under the fig tree when you need to, but when the Master
comes, be ready to go.
The Master will give you tasks that will utterly amaze you.

>"Very truly, I tell you, you will see heaven opened."
>(John 1:51)

Service

Jesus and the Good Old Boys

And he said to them, "Follow me, and I will make you fish for people."

Matthew 4:19

THE ACCLAIM AND PRESTIGE THAT WAS SO IMPORTANT IN THE BIG CITY
was not necessary for the proclamation of the good news.

When Jesus looked for men to be his disciples,
> he did not look for men with PhDs, MBAs, LLDs, or ThMs.

Jesus called a group of men who never thought they were good enough
    to be the disciples of the coming Messiah.

They were simply "good old boys."
They did what they did well but never thought of themselves as extraordinary.

Good old boys were exactly the kind of men Jesus asked to follow him.
He said, "Follow me, and I will make you fishers of men."
                              (Matthew 4:19)

He did not ask for perfection.
He asked for commitment.

Those fishermen recognized that Jesus believed in them,
    and that was all they needed to know.

Jesus believes in us,
    and that is all we need to know.

Together, Jesus and good old boys (and girls)
    can do what needs to be done.

Watch Out

Pentecost Sunday

"But you will be baptized with the Holy Spirit not many days from now."

Acts 1:5

Being in the Spirit is dangerous.

Stephen Cook

IT MAKES YOU DO THINGS YOU DO NOT NORMALLY DO.
It makes you love people who are not lovable.
It makes you seek God's heart to help you move forward.

Do not resist the leading of the Spirit.
Do not limit the power of the Holy Spirit.
Do not be afraid that you might be "Pentecostal."

The Spirit is moving!
And he might catch you.
And who knows what you might do?

Watch out!

Washed Feet

---

*Then he poured water into a basin and began
to wash the disciples' feet.*

John 13:5

HAVE YOU EVER CONSIDERED THE FEET OF
THE DISCIPLES?
Men who had lived their entire lives in sandals (when they were
not barefooted).
Men with crooked, misshapen, broken toes.
Men with calloused, flat, ugly feet.

Feet encrusted with the dust and grime of an arid land.
Feet that had been cut by sharp stones and pierced by briars.
Feet that had been smashed by many dropped loads.

And when those feet had been washed and dried with a towel,
>   they were still scarred,
>   and the toes were still broken and crooked,
>   but they were clean,
>   and they had been loved by the Savior.

And what did they do with their washed feet?
>   They took them to the garden.
>   Peter took his to a fire pit in a courtyard.
>   John took his to the cross.
>   Peter and John took theirs to an empty tomb.
>   The eleven hid theirs in a locked room.
>   One hundred and twenty took theirs to an upper room.

And then what happened?
>   Feet began to move.
>   They moved into the uttermost parts of the earth.
>   But the fact that their feet had been washed by the creator of the universe
>   > did not bring them peace.
>   It brought them pain.
>   They were imprisoned, tortured, abused, and martyred!

But the gospel!
>   The gospel went to Antioch.
>   The gospel went to Cyprus.
>   The gospel went to Thessalonica.
>   The gospel went to Corinth.
>   The gospel went to Ephesus.
>   The gospel went to Rome!

And we,
>	with our brokenness
>	and scars
>	and misshapen parts,
Are also loved by the Son of God.

Let us be off with our shoes.
Off with our pride.
Off with our arrogance.

Let us surrender our feet—
Yea, our lives—
To the humble Jesus.

Let us walk in the way that he has trod
>	and be a servant to all those who need us.

Grace

Every man according as he purposeth in his heart, so let him give.... And God is able to make all grace abound toward you.

2 Corinthians 9:7-8 KJV

STEWARDSHIP IS NOT A GIVING PROBLEM.
It is a grace problem.

We must come to terms with the fact that it is grace that has brought us this far.

Since God has given his all—
How much in all fairness can we keep for ourselves?

Grace that is greater than all our sin leads us to give all that we have.

It is not a giving problem.
It is a grace problem.

Doing

*If I speak in the tongues of mortals and of angels,
but do not have not love...I am nothing.*

1 Corinthians 13:1-2

*Earl Weaver, who was the manager of the Baltimore Orioles,
was famous, or infamous, for his arguments with the umpire.
One time he got right up in the face of the umpire and said,
"Are you going to get any better, or is this it?" And that,
of course, got him thrown out of the game.*

Stephen Cook

It does not matter what you say,
>   or what you do,
>   or what you give.
If it is not done in love,
>   it is worthless.

We will never get it exactly right,
>   but we must do what we do in the love of Christ.

It is not being in love.
It is doing in love.
It is not about doing church.
It is about doing love.

It is not about doing it in here.
It is about doing it out there.

If we are going to get any better doing the love of God,
>   we are going to have to get out there and do it.

Who Is Calling?

*Now the L*ORD *came and stood there, calling as before, "Samuel! Samuel!" And Samuel said, "Speak, for your servant is listening."*

1 Samuel 3:10

WHICH VOICE DO YOU LISTEN TO?
What does God's voice sound like?
What if you hear a voice but don't know who it is?

That is what faith is all about.
That is when you wait in silence.
That is when you empty yourself and let the Holy Spirit fill the void.

And when you are filled,
        you go.
Go with confidence.
Go filled with the Spirit.

But it is not easy to wait.
It is painful to empty yourself.
Lord, purge me of self-righteousness.

I am ready to go.
Call me.
Send me.

Unity

*Now the whole group of those who believed were
of one heart and soul.*

Acts 4:32

Unity in the midst of diversity.

The question is the strength of purpose.
The glue is the joy of the resurrection.
The call is to serve in the kingdom.
The fuel is the drive to minister to others.
The passion is to welcome all people.
The mission is to serve at this time in this place.
The task is to tear down the walls.

One heart.
One soul.
One baptism.
One salvation.
One Lord.
One God.

Unity in the midst of diversity.

The Gift

*But Peter said, "I have no silver or gold,
but what I have I give you; in the name of Jesus of Nazareth,
stand up and walk."*

Acts 3:6

THE GOOD NEWS IS THAT THERE IS ALWAYS AN
OPPORTUNITY FOR GRACE.
The blessing of God is that his grace is with us in all of life.

None of it is about us.
It is all about a loving God.

There is no boundary for God's grace.
God's grace is given freely to every person.
It is given to us so that we might scatter and give it to others.
Give it to every person, regardless of merit.

"Jumping up, he stood and began to walk, and he entered the temple with them, walking and leaping and praising God."
(Acts 3:8)

Be Careful

*Take care that you do not forget the L*ORD *your God.*

Deuteronomy 8:11

BE CAREFUL:
>That when you have forgotten about the manna,
>>you do not forget who provided it.

Be careful:
>That when you have become self-sufficient,
>>you do not forget those who supported you.

Be careful:
>That when the land of milk and honey is commonplace,
>>you do not forget who provided the victory.

Be careful:
>That when you have achieved your dreams and aspirations,
>>you do not forget that God is the giver of all good things.

Be careful:
>That you do not forget who you are.
>That you do not forget whose you are.

Stones of Remembrance

Be strong and courageous; do not be frightened or dismayed, for the LORD your God is with you wherever you go.

Joshua 1:9

Select twelve men from the people, one from each tribe, and command them, "Take twelve stones… carry them over with you."

Joshua 4:2-3

THE CHILDREN OF ISRAEL GATHERED STONES TO ESTABLISH A PLACE TO REMEMBER.
They had traveled
>from the demand of Moses' "Let my people go!"
>to the splashing of sandals across the Jordan.
And now it was time to move on.

Let the story remain.
Let the fellowship continue.
Let the vision go forth.

Gather strength from the past.
Gird up for the battle ahead.
Engage the future with courage.

There is work to be done.
There are battles to be won.
The past is the foundation,
But the future is the place for victory.

Change

*In the time of King Herod, after Jesus was born
in Bethlehem of Judea, wise men from the East came to Jerusalem,
asking, "Where is the child who has been born king of the Jews?
For we observed his star at its rising, and have come
to pay him homage." When King Herod heard this,
he was frightened, and all Jerusalem with him.*

Matthew 2:1-3

AND ALL JERUSALEM WITH HIM.
Nobody was looking for radical change.
Nobody wanted to upset the apple cart.

Sometimes change cannot happen because we are not looking for change.
The wise men not only saw the star;
They followed it.

Most people are not even looking for a star.
Most people do not want the intrusion of an outsider,
> especially if the intruder brings change.

There is trouble enough simply to maintain the status quo.
It takes courage to look for the opportunity to serve God
in new ways.

What might happen if we start interacting with the people
around us in new ways?
With a new attitude?
With open eyes?
Looking for a new way to serve?
Looking for a new ministry?

Change might happen!

Easter People

*They worshiped him, and returned
to Jerusalem with great joy.*

Luke 24:52

THE DISCIPLES WERE FILLED WITH GREAT JOY.
They had become Easter people.

Easter people are filled with great joy.
Easter people worship the risen Christ.
Easter people are becoming more than they ever were before.
Easter people are grounded in the grand purpose of God.
Easter people go out to share and to serve.

Easter people are a changing people.
Easter people are becoming more than they ever were before.
Easter people are grounded in the grand purpose of God.
Easter people go out to share and to serve.

The Cross

Standing near the cross of Jesus were his mother, and his mother's sister, Mary the wife of Clopas, and Mary Magdalene.

John 19:25

Many are willing to follow Jesus to the cross.
Few are willing to follow Jesus on the cross.

"Take up thy cross and follow me" is more than the road
to Golgotha.
It is the road to death.

There are many who would be willing to die
> for the sins of the world
>> if they knew they would rise from the dead in three days.
Even I would do that!

Jesus went to the cross to die,
> and he did die.

> "Unto thy hands I commit my spirit."
>> (Luke 23:46)

He gave up control.
He emptied himself.
He ventured into the unknown.

He predicted that he would rise on the third day,
> but he had to die to find out for sure.

There is no salvation without sacrifice.

Take Off Your Shoes

"I must turn aside and look at this great sight, and see why the bush is not burned up."

Exodus 3:3

DO WE SEE THE MYSTERY?
Do we recognize the unusual?
Do we watch carefully?

It was not that the bush was burning.
It was that the bush was not consumed.

Elizabeth Barrett Browning said,
> "Earth's crammed with heaven,
> And every common bush afire with God,
> But only he who sees takes off his shoes;
> The rest sit around and pick blackberries."

(From "Aurora Leigh" by Elizabeth Barnett Browning)

God did not speak until Moses stopped,
> and the message came after he took off his shoes.

God shows up in the "right now" if we are alert.
God is a God of interruption.
God is a God of disturbance.
God is a God of invasion.

Are we so comfortable
> in the mundane tending of our sheep
> that we do not know when to take off our shoes?

Waiting

"*Keep awake therefore, for you know neither the day nor the hour.*"

Matthew 25:13

Do you remember hide and seek? Here I come, ready or not.

Stephen Cook

Oh, the places you'll go.

Dr. Seuss

EVERYONE IS WAITING.
The question is, "What are we waiting for?"
What do you do while you are waiting?

One thing is to keep an adequate supply of oil.
Keep listening for the shout of his coming.

In the meantime be sure you have what you need for living this day.
Use the fuel you have.
Do not worry about when he will come.

> *We don't know when Jesus will come, but he will always come on time.* (Alex Haley, as quoted by Roger Lovette)

Carefully

Simon's mother-in-law was in bed with a fever, and they told him about her at once. He came and took her by the hand and lifted her up. Then the fever left her.

Mark 1:30-31

Care deeply, and deal carefully.

Stephen Cook

Jesus ministered to all kinds of people with all kinds of needs.
Regardless of the circumstances,
> he dealt carefully and cared deeply for all who needed him.

The responsibility to deal carefully must be constant in our ministry to others.
Sometimes that is not easy.
Sometimes hurt and frustration get in the way.
Sometimes we must plow our way through anger before we get to carefully.

The key is to care deeply.
Sometimes caring is more intellectual than it is emotional.
Deep caring is a mental discipline that must be molded in prayer and meditation.

Grant that we can care deeply and deal carefully with those who need us,
> just as Jesus cared for Peter's mother-in-law.

The Mantle

*He took the mantle of Elijah that had fallen from him,
and struck the water.*

2 Kings 2:14

Elijah's mantle was just a cloak until he struck the water with it.
It was still a cloak when it fell to Elisha.
It was still a cloak when he picked it up.

Elijah threw it down.
Elisha picked it up.

What do you do with it, Elisha?
Use it!
Strike the water with it!
It did not become an instrument of power for Elisha until
he struck the water with it.

Walk across the river into the service God has planned for you.
Grant that when the mantle is thrown, we have the courage to pick it up.
Grant that when we have it in our hands, we have the courage to use it.

The Plan

"Go into the village ahead of you...you will find tied there a colt... untie it and bring it."

Mark 11:2

Why?
Why find a colt?
Why was the colt ready?

Could it be that Jesus had a plan?
Could it be that the disciples did not have to know all the details?
Could it be that their job was to do what they were asked to do?

Sometimes there is no way for us to know exactly why.
Sometimes it is only much later, if ever, that we know why.
Sometimes we have to wait for revelation.

The truth is that we do not have to know.
The truth is that we simply have to act on faith.
The truth is that we may never know why we did what needed to be done.

God does not promise complete understanding.
Otherwise, faith would have no meaning.
God expects obedience.
God expects action.

God, help us.

Abide

Abide in me as I abide in you.

John 15:4

"Abide" is a beautiful word.

Stephen Cook

Contemporary couples use the word *unit*.
"We were good friends, but we were never a *unit*."
A British rock band has an album, *We Are a Unit*.

The New Revised Standard Version uses the word *abide*.
Live with me.
Reside with me.
Or even more profound,
    abide *in* me.

Let your spirit and the Holy Spirit commingle like two gases in a bottle.
You do not know where one starts and the other stops.

The Spirit dwells within and strives with you to face the difficulties of life.
You never have to struggle alone.
The sustaining power of the Holy Spirit is with you always.

And not only does the Holy Spirit provide power to the Christian.
He provides the same power to other Christians,
      and that combined power is called *church*.

Errrrbody

Now there were devout Jews from every nation under heaven living in Jerusalem.... But Peter, standing with the eleven, raised his voice and addressed them... "Then everyone who calls on the name of the Lord shall be saved."

Acts 2:5, 14, 21

In Memphis speak, Peter said, "ERRRRBODY."

Stephen Cook

Every time we struggle with the question
"Who is in, and who is out?"
> we come up against Peter's statement.

Everyone.

Let's face it.
The church is inefficient because it has great imperfections.

It includes us, all of us,
> with all of our faults,
> with all of our prejudices,
> with all of our fears,
> with all of our failures,
> with all of our doubts,
> with all of the negative things that fill our lives.

But we all have a place at God's table.

> "For God so loved the world [EVERYBODY] that he gave his only Son."
> (John 3:16)

Beyond Z

Now the LORD *said to Abram,
"Go from your country and your kindred and your
father's house to the land that I will show you."*

Genesis 12:1

On beyond Z there is truth that is more than the truth we know.

Stephen Cook

My alphabet starts where your alphabet ends.

Dr. Seuss, *On Beyond Zebra!*

GO, ABRAM, GO.
Go where?
He did not know.
But he went anyway.

When you get to the end of your dreams.
When you are beyond the sum of your success.
Why would you want to change?
Why would you want to go?

It is not a matter of wanting to change.
It is the matter of the voice of God.
How long does it take to know it is the voice of God?
If you wait until you know, why is faith required?

> "By faith Abraham obeyed when he was called and set out for a place that he was to receive as an inheritance; and he set out, not knowing where he was going."
> (Hebrews 11:8)

Go beyond Z to new letters you have never known.
Let God expand your horizons to new lands.
Go beyond the truth you think you know.
Go beyond the relationships you are comfortable with.

God is always calling you to go beyond,
    to reach out to others,
    to take the risky path,
    to love the unlovely.

Go, Christian, go.
Go where?
Out there, beyond Z.
Out there in the world of new truth!

www.ingramcontent.com/pod-product-compliance
Lightning Source LLC
Chambersburg PA
CBHW070843160426
43192CB00012B/2296